# Dan Coates
# Popular Music Collection
## For The Advanced Player
### VOLUME II

## CONTENTS


Angel Eyes. . . 48
Because You Loved Me. . . 16
Beauty And The Beast. . . 6
Canon In D (Pachelbel). . . 36
Desperado. . . 20
A Dream Is A Wish Your Heart Makes. . . 24
Heart. . . 28
Hey, There. . . 32
If You Believe. . . 11
Send In The Clowns. . . 40
Un-break My Heart. . . 2
Valentine. . . 44



Project Manager: Carol Cuellar
Cover Design: Ken Rehm

# UN-BREAK MY HEART

Words and Music by
DIANE WARREN
*Arranged by DAN COATES*

(legato)
simile
cresc. poco a poco
mf
3
3

To Coda
f
decresc.
1.
2.
mp
mp
mf
cresc.
D.S. al Coda
f

Coda
f
cresc.
ff
meno mosso
f
rit.
mf
8va
p
3

*From Walt Disney's "BEAUTY AND THE BEAST"*

# BEAUTY AND THE BEAST

Lyrics by
HOWARD ASHMAN

Music by
ALAN MENKEN
*Arranged by DAN COATES*

p
mp
3
3
3
mf
mp
mf

f
cresc.
ff
f
meno mosso
mf rall.
mp a tempo
cresc.
mf
mp

p
mf
f
mf decresc.
sfz
rit.
3
f a tempo
mf cresc.

f
mf
mp
meno mosso
p
rit.
mp a tempo
p
rit. e dim.
pp

# IF YOU BELIEVE

Composed by
JIM BRICKMAN
*Arranged by DAN COATES*

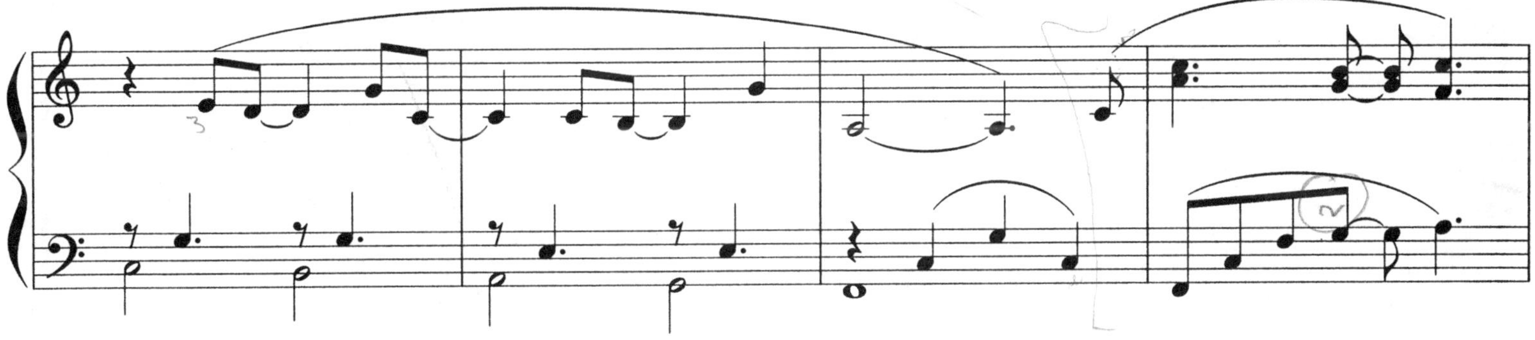

1.
mf
2.
mf
mp cresc.

mf
sf
mp
mf
sf
mp
cresc.
mf
f rit. e dim.

mp a tempo
cresc. poco a poco
mf
f
dim.
rit.
8va
mf a tempo

mf
f
mf
dim.
mp
mf rit.
Tempo ad lib.
f
meno mosso
rit.
fz

# BECAUSE YOU LOVED ME
## (Theme from "Up Close & Personal")

Words and Music by
DIANE WARREN
*Arranged by DAN COATES*

mf
cresc.
f
mf legato
f

To Coda
1.
mf
dim.
mp
2.
mf
cresc. poco a poco
f
ff
3
D.S. al Coda
mf

Coda
f
cresc.
3
3
ff
decresc.
mf
mp
meno mosso
p

# DESPERADO

Words and Music by
DON HENLEY and GLEN FREY
*Arranged by DAN COATES*

mp
cresc.
mf

1.
f
mf
3
dim.
mp
2.
8va
mf
decresc.
mp
8vb
mf
8vb

cresc.
3
3
f
ff
mf
rit.
mp a tempo
8va
p
pp

*From Walt Disney's "CINDERELLA"*

# A DREAM IS A WISH YOUR HEART MAKES

Words and Music by
MACK DAVID, AL HOFFMAN
and JERRY LIVINGSTON
*Arranged by DAN COATES*

mp
3
3
8va
mf
8vb
poco accerlerando
meno mosso
rit.

f a tempo
dim.
legato
mp
rit.
fz
mp
cresc. poco a poco
mf
8va
ff
8va
8va
decresc.
8va
mf

Slower
rit. e dim.
mp
cresc.
mf
rall.
mp
meno mosso
8va
8va
p
molto rit.
pp
ppp

From the Broadway Musical Production "DAMN YANKEES"

# HEART

Words and Music by
RICHARD ADLER and JERRY ROSS
*Arranged by DAN COATES*

8va
mp
mf
(8va)
loco
8va
mp
p
mf

f
mf
mp
mf
cresc.
f
8va
loco
mf

1.
mp
mp
3
3
3
3
3
4
5

3
3
3

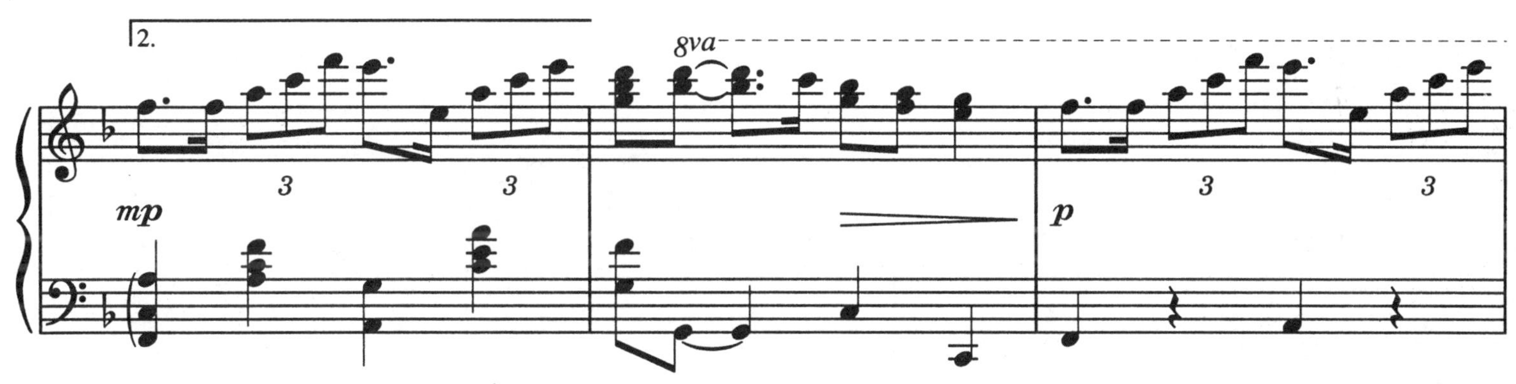
2.
8va
mp
p
3
3
3
3

(8va)
loco
8va
pp
mf
3
3
3
3
3
3
3
3

From the Broadway Musical Production "THE PAJAMA GAME"

# HEY THERE

Words and Music by
RICHARD ADLER and
JERRY ROSS
*Arranged by DAN COATES*

**Moderately slow "swing" feel** ♩ = 76

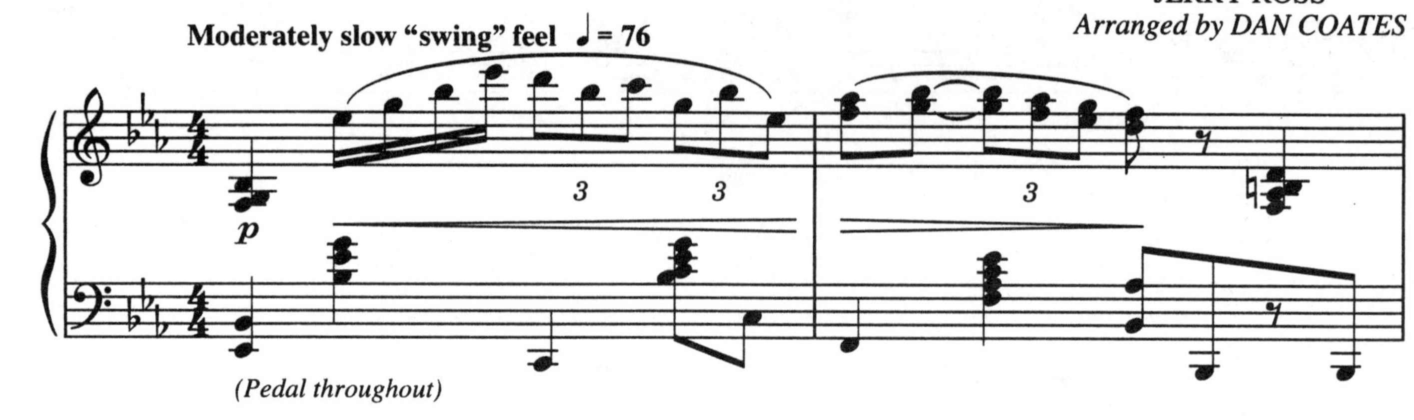

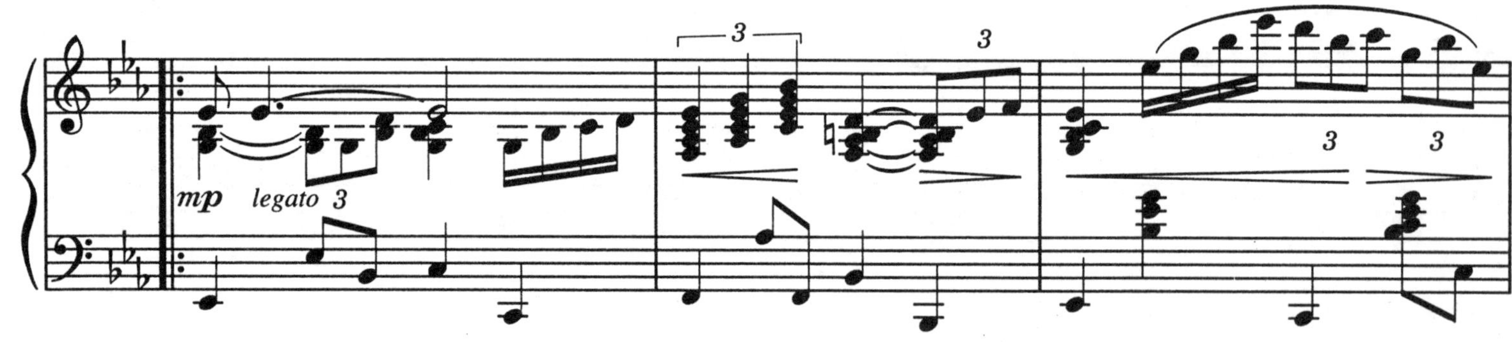

8va
mf
cresc.
f
mf
8va
mp

8va
mf
3
cresc.
f
ff
6
decresc.

8va
mp
(8va)
mf
f
mp
1.
8va
mp
2.
(No swing tempo)
rall.
mp
p

# CANON IN D

JOHANN PACHELBEL
(1653-1706)
*Arranged by DAN COATES*

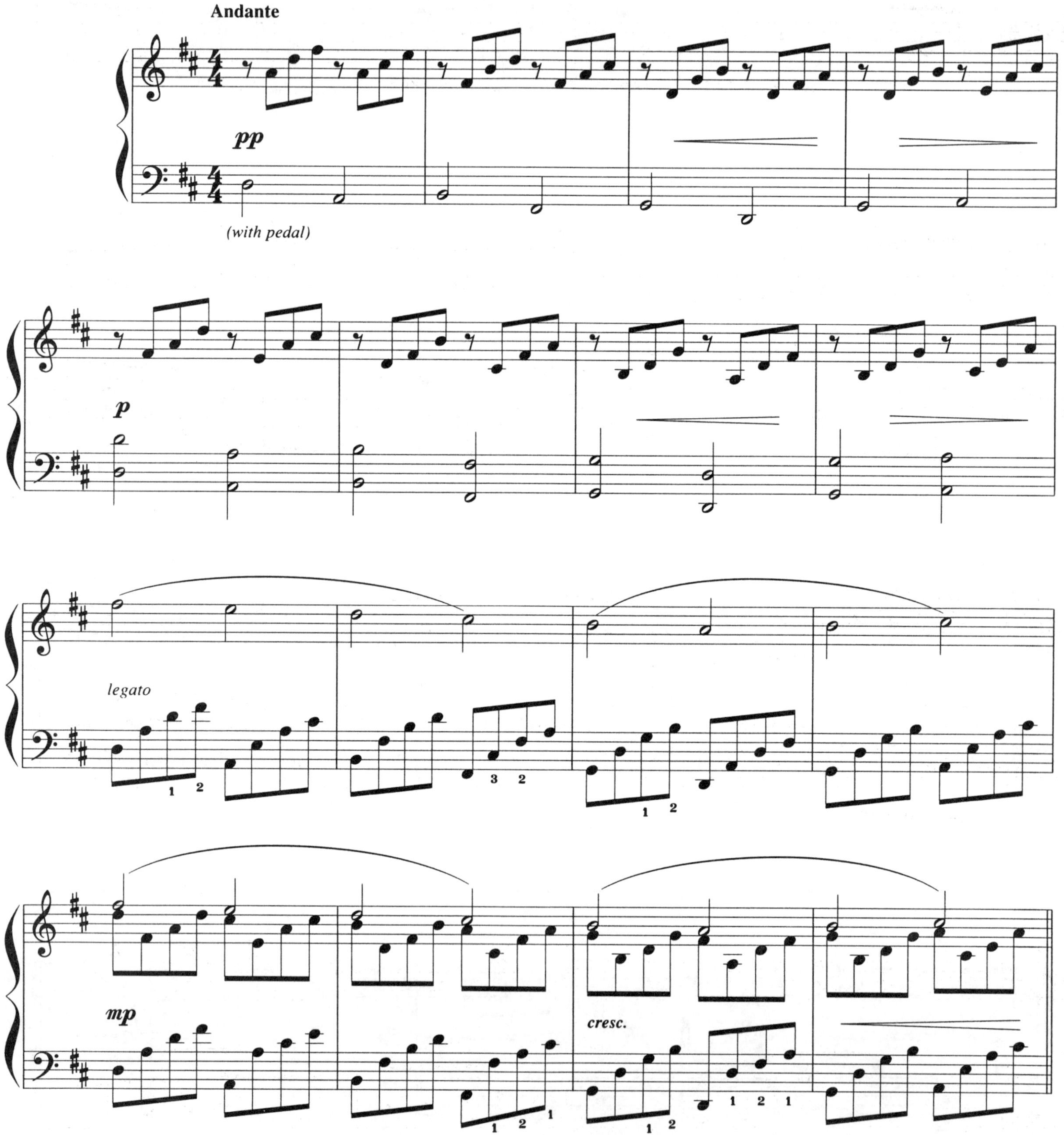

mf
mp
cresc.
mf

cresc. poco a poco
f
3
4
3
1
1
3
1
2
1
5
4
1
cresc.
1
8va

8va
ff
dim.
f
mf
mp
decresc. poco a poco
p
rit. e dim.
pp

From the Broadway Musical Production "A LITTLE NIGHT MUSIC"

# SEND IN THE CLOWNS

Music and Lyrics by
STEPHEN SONDHEIM
*Arranged by DAN COATES*

a tempo
mf
f
mf decresc.
mp cresc.
mf
f

mf
dim. e rit.
mp a tempo
2
2
2
2
2
rit.
8va
loco
a tempo
cresc.
poco rit.
a tempo
f
2

f
mf
decresc.
mp
1.
cresc.
2.
poco rit.
mp
a tempo
rit.
8va
p
pp

# VALENTINE

Composed by
JIM BRICKMAN
*Arranged by DAN COATES*

**Moderately slow** (♩ = 92)

*p* *legato*

*mp*

cresc.
mf
3
dim.
mp

1.
p
2.
mp
3
cresc.
mf
3
3
f
3

mf
dim.
mp
rit. e dim.
p
a tempo
rit.
pp

# ANGEL EYES

Composed by
JIM BRICKMAN
*Arranged by DAN COATES*

mp
cresc.
mf
f
mf
dim.
(R.H.)
5
5
(L.H.)

mp
cresc. poco a poco
f
mf

f
dim.
8va
mp
mf
mp

cresc.
mf
mp
rit.
mf a tempo
cresc.
f